THE *Return* OF

Jesus Christ

The Final Hour

THE Return OF Jesus Christ

The Final Hour

ADRIENNE F. MANSON

Pleasant W*rd

ISBN 1-4141-0428-6
Library of Congress Catalog Card Number: 2005901946

Dedication

I thank the Lord Jesus Christ for the inspiration that He gave me in writing this book. For without God it Could not have been accomplished.

Table of Contents

Introduction

"For the Lord himself shall descend from heaven with a shout, with the voice of the archangel, and with the trump of God; and the dead in Christ shall rise first."

—*I Thess. 4:16*

This is the scripture most referred to when the return of Jesus Christ is in discussion. Throughout the content of this book you will notice the phrase the last hour, it refers to this day and time in which we all currently live. Some consider Jesus' return as a big He-Ho or some type of fantasy out of a storybook. Many are unaware that Jesus Christ is soon to come. But yet many believers a wait in the expectation of our Lord and Savior Jesus Christ.

My dear beloved friends of unbelief I write to inform you and awaken you. I also write to sound the alarm, and to blow the trumpet in Zion. It is also a warning to the unbeliever in hope to enlighten him/her of the return of Jesus Christ, the only Messiah.

In this last hour there will be last day ministries released within the earth that will advance the kingdom of God to a whole new level, a level that will operate and function like a well oiled machine. A level that will be well capable of recognizing the very presence and essence of the enemy, at a level that will sniff out the enemy's camp like a bloodhound, and will advance, and not retreat. At a level that is not afraid to invade the enemy's camp to seize, takeover, to overthrow the enemy's kingdom, snatching lost souls from the flames of hell.

At a level that is not afraid to tell the dope man this corner no longer belongs to you it belongs to God now repent and receive your salvation. At a level that will function and operate to carry the manifested presence and power of God every they go. See yourself taking the presence of God with you and operating while shopping as you push your grocery buggy down the isle those that pass by you will be healed of their ailments.

And it is not operating at a level where you will take 20-30 minutes to work up a prayer. Your very presence will carry the manifested presence of God to a degree and measure that will touch all those who come in contact with you. It's the Glory of the Lord that I am speaking of, and it is his Glory that will be operating through you my children. But know this, this level is only for those who believe, consecrate, sanctify, and separate themselves apart from the world.

Just like Joshua told the people in Joshua 3:5 told the people sanctify yourselves for on tomorrow the Lord will do wonders among you. There is a move of God being birthed in the nation that has not been seen since the days of Azusa. My dear beloved children God is preparing his people for a profound move, a powerful move, a move that mere earthly words can not describe; a move that will wake millions who are deeply spiritually asleep. But we need some intercessors; are there any willing and committed who will weep between the porch and the altar.

Let me put it another way; church it is time to get into a priestly position, sanctify yourself, put on holiness, separate yourself for a special holy purpose for such a time as this.

Chapter 1

....

The Last Hour

L et us not be as it were in the days of Noah right before the flood.   Let us now take a look at the Scripture.

'The earth also was corrupt before God, and the Earth was filled with violence. And God looked upon the earth, and, behold, it was corrupt; for all flesh had corrupted his way upon the earth. And God said unto Noah, THE END OF ALL FLESH IS COME BEFORE ME: for the earth is filled with violence through them; and, behold, I will destroy with the earth."

—*Genesis 6:11-13*

We will take a look at the day of Noah in comparison to the last hour.   Now as we look at this particular Scripture notice the highlighted text. My friend God makes this statement. This was not a decision of Noah, nor anyone else that was (hanging out at that time). Now the two words last hour can apply to that time right before the flood. It was the last hour for all flesh at that time.

Now, for all the skeptics and critics who always say well show me where the Bible says God actually destroyed all flesh. Okay let us now look at Genesis 7:21-23.

> *"And all flesh died that moved upon the earth, both of fowl, and of cattle, and of beast, and of every creeping thing that creepeth upon the earth, and every man; All in whose nostrils was the breath of life, of all that was in the dry land, died. And every living substance was destroyed which was upon the face of the ground, both man, and cattle, and the creeping things, and the fowl of the heaven; and they were destroyed from the earth: and Noah only remained alive, and they that were with him in the ark."*

Now then, to answer your question. Some of you want to know well why was Noah left alive. Noah was a just man, and he walked with God. In the day of Noah's last hour there was much violence and corruption in the land. (My dear friends the end of all flesh is near in this last hour, (for the unsaved).

Many years make up this last hour. No man knows the day or time when Jesus will return. But the Messiah does put urgency in the spirit of his people to let them know the kingdom of God is at hand.

In the day of John the Baptist he went about preaching "repent, for the kingdom of God is at hand". Beloved I say unto you, "repent, for the Kingdom of God is at hand". To simplify the whole matter, there was sin and corruption in the land in the day of Noah. Which brings us to the real reason why flesh was destroyed. SIN.

Beloved ones sin is what separates man from God. As long as there is sin in an individual life you won't find God in that person's life. God's whole purpose for making man was not for him to sin, but that he would praise and magnify God. Let's deal with that for a moment. Sin, an act or practice of ungodliness, uncleanness, (such as homosexuality, drunkenness, witchcraft, and practicing the occult).

Let's take another look at an example of a last hour. The land of Sodom and Gomorrah. Genesis 19:23-25.

> *"The sun was risen upon the earth when Lot entered into Zoar. Then the Lord rained upon Sodom and upon Gomorrah brimstone and fire from the Lord out of heaven; and he over-*

threw those cities, and all the plain, and all
the inhabitants of the cities, and that which
grew upon the ground."

In the last hour of Sodom and Gomorrah there was much wickedness and sin in the land, (much fornication). The meaning of the term "last hour" for this day and time is equal to the same meaning right before the coming of the Lord. To give you a good description of "last hour" means right before the rapture.

The only individuals who will escape the tribulation after the last hour (or one can say after the rapture if you like) are the ones who have accepted Jesus Christ and lived for him. This world in which we live is in the last hour.

"This know also also, that in the last days Peril-
ous times shall come. For men shall be lovers
of their Own selves, covetous, boasters, proud,
blasphemers, Disobedient to parents, unthank-
ful, unholy,"

—II Timothy 3:1-2

No one has to think twice to wonder if any of the above things are prevalent in our society today. The Word of God clearly states that in the last days perilous times shall come; beloved ones are we not in hard times? The Lord is merciful, for he always gives a warning to evildoers of wickedness before he lets his wrath come upon anyone. In each situation there is one common factor, it is apparent that man's corrupt ways brought down the wrath of God. As in this last hour mankind have become very corrupt, there will be a rapture of the church and then the wrath of God will take place which will be the tribulation period. My friend don't wait around get SAVED TODAY, and live for God.

Let's make a comparison with Noah, and Sodom and Gomorrah. There was much evil in both lands, what happen Jehovah God had to put a stop to all the wickedness. This nation is about to experience one of the greatest moves of God ever seen. The power of God will be manifested in degrees that the world hasn't seen in decades. Restoration, God is going to restore in this last hour. Restoration to broken-hearts will be mended back together, homes restored, marriages will be put back together. There will come a tremendous flow in the spirit in our church services. Miracles will take place like never before. There is an anointing that God is pouring out on his people for the work of the last day's ministries. God is anointing and appointing his people to various and specific duties to be carried out in this last hour.

In this last hour the Word of God will be preached, and preached to thousands, upon thousands. Men and women everywhere will be saved. The church will begin to see true men and women of God expound on the Word in such a way that you have never seen. Revelation knowledge of God's Word will be opened up to man in a deeper understanding. You will see the men/women who have practiced in the occult turn their hearts toward God. People that have practiced witchcraft will pour into the churches seeking help. Sorcery users, warlocks, the astrology reader, psychic readers will come out of their houses, and will have a hunger to know God.

Jehovah God is forming a mighty army that will consist of all races, creeds and denominations. God's great army is in the process of being formed even as you read these words. God's great army refers to his glorious church, because his glorious church is his army. Now understand the concept of the glorious church. Let's look at Ephesians 5:27.

> *"That he might present it to himself a glorious church not having spot, or wrinkle, or any such thing: but that it should be holy and without blemish."*

In order for God to form his army, there must first come a purging of the church. Anything that's unholy or unclean will be purged out. There will be no murmuring, division, strife, bitterness, unforgiveness, envy, gossip or rioting among the people of God.

The spirit of God is moving throughout all churches across the nation. The church (The body of Christ) is in a preparation stage. Getting prepared for the coming of the Lord: Let's use this analogy, there are certain changes that a bride will go through before their wedding day. A bride wants to make sure everything is perfect and in place before that great day the bride wants her garments to be immaculately clean before coming down the isle.

Now in the realm of the spirit Christ has his church in the preparation stages of becoming immaculately clean. Thus the glorious church is that one body that consists of all denominations, and races. The walls of partition are coming down between denominations. In this last hour there is a rude awakening to all those who figure only their faith of doctrine will make it in.

In regard to finances for the last hour, the people of God will experience abundance in their finances in this last hour. The people of God shall be blessed like never before in this Last Hour, humble people of God are going to be exalted. Some individuals will experience for the first time owning their own businesses. Major corporations will crumble and fall to replaced by godly corporations. The systems of this world will soon come to a complete stop. This is why the people of God must learn to operate on God's system and stop operating on the world's system. It is utterly important to really learn the spiritual laws and principles of sowing and reaping.

The more people of God trust God, the more they will experience God moving in their behalf. The people of God will be ushered into a new threshold of faith. The Lord wants to open up new avenues and doors unto his people.

Joshua 1:8 reads

"This book of the law shall not depart out of thy mouth; but thou shalt meditate therein day and night, that thou mayest observe to do according to all that is written therein: for then thou shall make thy way prosperous, then thou shall have good success."

The bible said thou, (thou means you) you have to meditate, that you may observe, then you shall make your way prosperous, and then you shall have good success. Beloved ones you must make the first step. Launch out into the deep, and let down your nets for a draught (Luke 5:4). It's up to the individual to make that decision if he/she wants to live out this Last Hour in defeat or victory. God wants his people to live in total victory in the Last Hour.

Now I must warn those Christians who are living in carnality and being lukewarm. GET IT TOGETHER! If you are a cold, carnal or lukewarm Christian I plead and beg of you to get the baptism in the HOLY GHOST. I plead with you to get out of your flesh and begin walking in the spirit of God. Those Christians who are walking in carnality, the way will be made hard for you. In this last hour the prayers of the carnal minded Christians will go unanswered for long periods of time. Carnal Christians will go long periods of time before they even begin to receive any type of breakthrough. The bible says in Romans 8:6-8

> *"For to be carnally minded is death; but to be spiritually minded is life and peace. Because the carnal mind is enmity against God: For it is not subject to the law of God, neither indeed can be. So then they that are in the flesh cannot please God."*

If you are a carnal Christian, and have never heard of a rude awakening, then you soon will experience one. This Scripture in Romans will come to life in many hearts of believers that are living in carnality. For so many years some believers have walked in carnality, but the clock is about to stop ticking. My friend you are dying a slow death, and you don't know it because you aren't in the spirit and you can't see what satan is doing. The Scripture says in:

> *"So then because thou art lukewarm, and Neither cold nor hot, I will spew thee out of my mouth."*
>
> —*Revelation 3:16*

In all actuality this is certainly a warning to lukewarm believers. In the days of the last hour the type of walk that you have with the Lord is about to tell. In this last hour covers are coming off and many things are about to be revealed to God's people. Our Lord and Savior Jesus Christ wants to talk to his people and he is talking to his people, but only those who are walking in the spirit. The Bible says in Galatians 5:25

> *"If we live in the spirit, let us also walk in the spirit."*

There are heavenly messages that our Jehovah God wants to give unto his people, but in order to receive those messages we as a people of god must walk in the spirit to hear the message, and then bring the message down from the heavenly to earth so that his kingdom may come in earth as it is heaven. (Matt. 6:10)

You see beloved ones there is a divine plan and purpose for every individual. In order to fulfill our purpose we must seek the kingdom, and to seek the kingdom is to seek the face of God.

It is my conviction that in this last hour it is God's perfect will for the Body of Christ to become unified in the spirit. His perfect will is that the body of Christ become as one. Remember:

> *"There is one body, and one spirit, even As ye are called in one hope of your calling; one Lord, One faith, one baptism, one God and Father of all, who Is above all, and through all, and in you all."*
>
> *—Ephesians 4:46*

Chapter 2

. . . .

The Demonic Realm in the Last Hour

"Be sober, be vigilant; because your adversary the devil, as a roaring lion, walketh about, seeking whom he may devour."

—*I Peter 5:8*

A gain, notice the highlighted text seeking whom he may devour. Seeking whom he may devour in illness, spirits of infirmity defeat destruction, discouragement and CARNAL-ITY. Beloved ones don't fall subject to satan's many tactics and loopholes. The scripture says as a roaring lion, it didn't say he was a roaring lion. People of God don's get fooled, know who you are in Christ Jesus, know that there is power in the blood of Jesus.

Know how to apply the blood of Jesus in every situation that satan uses to come against you.

Just saying the blood of Jesus won't accomplish what you need done. (Anyone can stand around screaming the Blood of Jesus). But when you know within your spirit, and know that at the name of Jesus every knee should bow. (Phil 2:10) And if you know that, if you submit to God and resist the devil and he will flee from you. (James 4:7) And if you know that the devils also believe, and tremble. (James 2:19). Then when satan comes around your front door and you say the BLOOD OF JESUS; the whole host of hell will tremble because you know that there really is power in the Blood. Beloved ones I never thought I was actually put this in print, but did you know the Blood of Jesus even works on dogs. There have been a time or two when a dog and I do mean a mean dog was running behind me and I turned to face the dog and I quickly said the Blood of Jesus and the dog did not bite me. The dog ran off trembling in fear.

Beloved ones we have entered into a day and time where it's going to take more than attending our Sunday morning worship service, sitting on the front pew saying, "amen Pastor", "preach the Word", and "help yourself preacher". It's going to take consecration, dedication to face to face. In this last

hour it is a must that you have a strong conviction.
In Ephesians 4:14

> *"That we henceforth be no more children, tossed
> to and fro, and carried about with every wind of
> doctrine, by the sleight of men, and cunning crati-
> ness, whereby they lie in wait to deceive;"*

The word says that we henceforth be no more
children, tossed to and from.   The Lord doesn't
want any one to fall into deception.   But there will
be many in this last hour that will, due to the hard-
ness of their heart.   They have turned a deaf ear to
the teachings of Jesus Christ.   That makes one an
open and direct target for the enemy to come and
lure you into deception of a false doctrine.

It's true that many homosexuals have come out
of the "closet".   Prepare yourselves my friends there
are many more to come.   Many will come preaching
Jesus and then announce they are a homosexual and
in agreement to the homosexual movement.

Many attacks will come upon the church body.
Not so much as physical, but attacks in the spirit
realm.   If there was ever a time to learn spiritual
warfare, beloved ones now is the time to prepare for
warfare.   Know that the people of God will not be
overtaken, for the Word says in Matt. 16:18:

"And I say also unto thee, that thou art Peter,
and upon this rock I will build my church; and the
gates of hell shall not prevail Against it."

The gates of hell shall not prevail against it. "It" meaning the church of the living God.   If you are part of the body of Christ then satan will not prevail against you. But the key to the whole matter my friend is to stand on the rock (stand on the Word).

Though there may come attacks, know that the people of God will be knit together in love, the Word says in Colossians 2:2

"That their hearts might be comforted, being
knit together in love, and unto all riches of full
assurance of understanding, the acknowledge-
ment of the mystery of God, and of Father, and
of Christ;"

There will be unification in the spirit amongst the body of Christ, no matter what race, or denomination, God wants his people united together in love.   Many are unaware of satan's many tactics, my prayer for all of you is that the Jehovah God will give you revelation on how to act upon the defense magnetism that Jesus has given unto us.

My friends beware of psychic prayers, there are individuals that work in the occult and in witchcraft that use psychic prayers.   Let me explain to those that may not fully understand what a psychic prayer is. Beloved ones there are many people that you are unaware of that repeat demonic curses and prayers against you to weaken you very walk with God. The people of God may sometime experience a heavy spirit and don't understand what the problem may be. People may sometime feel that "there's a cloud hanging over my head" or "nothing ever goes right for me." My friend you may be experiencing some demonic interference. There isn't a cloud handing above your head, but you are under attack from satan.

What satan does to the saints of God, is try to slow them down so they won't pray. Satan uses his devil worshippers to say psychic prayers against saints to hinder their prayers. Beloved ones there are people that pray to satan night and day to keep us from praying and trying to keep our prayers from being answered. Witchcraft and satan worshippers are very real beloved one and yes they do have power, but they aren't an ounce of a match for OUR ALIGHTY GOD! To get a clear picture of the matter let's look at this passage of Scripture.

"Then said he unto me, fear not, Daniel: for from the first day that thou didst set thine heart to understand, and to chasten thyself before thy God, thy words were heard, and I am come for they words.

—*Daniel 9:12:13*

But the prince of the kingdom of Persia (satan) withstood me one and twenty days: (21) But, lo, Michael, one of the chief princes, came to help me: and I remained there with the kings of Persia."

My friends the fight is in the spirit realm of the heavenly. We can't see the battle with the natural eye, but there is a spiritual warfare going on every-day. Daniel fasted and prayed for 21 days. God had released the answer the first day, but it didn't manifest in the physical until 21 days later.

It is of extreme importance to have a prayer life. Let's took at Ephesians 6:12:

"For we wrestle not against flesh and blood, but against principalities, against powers, against the rulers of the darkness of this world, against spiritual wickedness in high places."

Many Christians don't understand or realize that there is a real warfare in the heavenly. The believers prayer life is what really determines and constitutes how victorious and how powerful your walk with God will be. There is much truth when they say little prayer, little power or much prayer, much power. So what do you do now, START PRAYING!!! Communicate with God, the more you spend time in the presence of almighty God you will begin to see drastic changes in your life. People of God know that you can walk in the Holy of Holies place, know that you can bring the Glory of God down into your life. You have to bring it down, which means reaching up in prayer, grab a hold onto God and let the Glory of the Lord reign in your life.

Remember *I Thessalonians 5:17: "Pray without ceasing."*

· ·

Chapter 3

Travailing In the Spirit

"Likewise the spirit also helpeth our Infirmities: for we know not what we should pray for As we ought: but the spirit itself maketh intercession for us with groanings which cannot be uttered.

And he that searcheth the hearts knoweth what is the mind Of the spirit, because he maketh intercession for the saints according to the will of God."

—*Romans 8:25-27*

C hurch, it is time to travail in prayer and intercession, it's time to weep between the porch and the altar. Many times there are ministries that need to be birth forth in prayer. Unless you seek the face of God it can't come into manifestation. Let's use this analogy: Just as a women in a delivery room ready to give birth to her child she travails with groaning and utterance that no one can understand the degree of pain that she feels at that moment.

Now then in the realm of the spirit, the church is in expectation of her Lord to come, but there are many things that must come forth before the coming of the Lord. There are ministries to be birthed out, there are prophesies that have went forth in the lives of people of God that are yet unfilled. Beloved ones we must pray intercede and trail so that these things may come to pass. Some of you are long, long overdue for some things that have been spoken over your lives. What has happened God spoke it, and you did believe it full-hearted when God spoke it. But as time goes by you slowly start loosing the faith and before you know it you have forgotten that God has promised to bless.

Start rebuking the adversary; don't allow him to hold things up in the heavenlies. God has already loosed it, but there is a need to rebuke the devil. Don't let satan steal from you. People of God, in this last hour it is time for great intercession and travailing in the spirit. There are great groans which cannot be uttered in the realm of the spirit. God needs somebody that will travail and intercede on the behalf of the church. God needs somebody He

can move and work through. Jehovah God is look-
ing for some yielded vessels that will pray and travail
that His glory may be revealed in this last hour.   If
there are no intercessors (Isa. 59:16) for the nations
how then can the work of God be accomplished to
its highest level.

Beloved ones let's focus on:

(1) Travailing
(2) The work of the ministry

Let's see how these go hand in hand.   There is
only one ministry, and that is the ministry of our
Lord and Savior Jesus Christ.   We all play a part in
this work.   There are many different functions and
operations, and are different functions and operations, and administrations, but only one ministry.
Christ is the head of the ministry, and we are the
body.

When there are intercessor ministries can be
birthed out into the fullness, without a breach in
the spirit or a premature birth.   God is in need
and in search of prayer warriors that will intercede
for countries like Africa, the Netherlands, Mexico,
Hawaii, Europe, Greece, etc. We are unaware of the
needs of these countries in the natural, but when
intercession takes place strongholds are broken.

There is a great need for intercession for infirmities of the people of God.   There is a great amount of

lack of knowledge among different members of the body. God needs those who are open to intercession to intercede for the part of the body that has a stunt growth in Christ that they may come to maturity in Christ. God desires to pour out wisdom, under-standing, and knowledge into his people. Ephesians 1:17-19 says:

> *"That the God of our Lord Jesus Christ, the Father of Glory, may give unto you the spirit of wisdom and revelation in the knowledge of him: The eyes of your understanding being enlightened; that ye may know what is the hope of his calling, and what the riches of the glory of his inheritance in the saints, and what is the exceeding greatness of his power to us ward who believe, according to the working of his mighty power,"*

People of God know your position, know that you have authority and power over satan. Know that you have authority as a believer.

> *Luke 10:19 says "behold, I give unto you power to tread on serpents and scorpions, and over all the power of the enemy: and nothing shall by any means hurt you."*

Jesus has given unto every believer power over the adversary. Know that your position is the posi-tion of an overcomer and a victorious winner, that my friend is your position. An overcomer and a

victorious winner.   Every believer has authority.
You have the right and authority to use the name
of Jesus in every situation, because you have been
redeemed by the precious blood of Jesus.

People of God; always use the Word of God.
One sure way of living victorious is to keep the Word
of God in your mouth.

> *"But what saith it? The word is nigh thee, even
> In thy mouth, and in thy heart: that is, the Word
> of faith, which We preach;"*

> —*Romans 10:8*

God moves and acts upon his word.   It is faith
and the Word that moves him.   My friend faith and
the Word are partners; it takes faith in the Word
of God to receive from God.   In this last hour it is
time to receive from God, time to abide in God, time
to walk in the Holy of Holies place.   God has no
respect of persons all believers are capable through
Jesus Christ our Lord to live victorious lives.   It's
time to intercede for the lost souls.   As the body of
Christ we must do as Matt. 11:12:

> *"And from the days of John the Baptist until now
> kingdom of heaven suffereth violence, and the
> violent take it by force."*

People of God know that you can take it force. Much intercession is also needed for infirmities in the natural. Satan is attacking many believers with illness and different diseases in their bodies. There is great work that can and will be accomplished through intercession. This last hour is a time of travailing in the spirit that God may have his divine way in the hearts and lives of the people of God all across the nations.

The church will witness many miraculous miracles. The Apostles performed many miracles. Beloved one get ready because through travailing and fasting, the body of Christ is about to experience a great move of God and an out pouring of the Spirit of God. The gifts of the spirit will be in full restoration through prayer.

In Galatians 5:25 "If we live in the spirit, let us also walk in the spirit."

Those that are sincerely walking in the spirit of God will experience new heights in God. God will use those that are truly led by the spirit of God. Those that are not afraid to walk in the realm of the spirit, God will use you to accomplish much kingdom work. There are babes in Christ who are in need of someone to stand in the gap for them. Intercession is needed that they will mature in Christ and that they will stand against the wiles of the devil.

Prayer is needed for them that the cares of this life will not choke the Word out of them. People of God it is time for intercession.

In this last hour the church will experience international ministries. Let me explain. There will be other ministries from across the continent that will come to the United States to minister and expound of the Word of God. The people of God have experienced international ministry but in this last hour it will become more common and there will come a large increase of international ministry.

Some of the ministries are coming to do a specific work; some are coming to teach in different areas that have not been touched on in the United States. They are coming to perfect, and up build the People of God in certain areas. Many men of God from the United States are going to travel to States they never thought it would be possible.

You see Jesus wants to bring his people out of this traditional way of worship that we have relaxed in and show us how other ministries flow in the spirit of God.

Chapter 4

* *

The Promises of God

"For all the promises of God in him are yea, and In him Amen, unto the glory of God by us."

—*II Corinthians 1:20*

How do we receive the promises of God? There are hundreds of promises, but how do we get the promises from the realm of the heavenly into the physical or natural realm. People of God know that it is for you personally. God has given it to you. It's a promise Jesus can't and won't take something back he has already given to you.

Once it has been established in our minds that the promises of God are meant for every believer as an individual then maybe we will start receiving the promises.   The promises of God already belong to you, you already own it. Think of it as being in your possession at this very moment.   In this last hour before the return of Jesus Christ the people of God will receive what God has promised unto us.

Our Lord and Savior Jesus Christ desires that you receive from him.   Beloved ones I can't stress how important it is for you to walk in the spirit in this last hour.   A lot depends on your church.   Believe that you are walking in the promises of God.   Someone may ask; what are the promises of God?

> *"If ye abide in me, and my words abide in you, ye Shall ask what ye will, and it shall be done unto you."*
>
> —*John 15:7*

Beloved ones this is only one promise.   Just by knowing this passage of scripture, as a believer you are able to walk in full confidence in Jesus knowing that what ever you ask shall be done unto you.   Next I would like to share with you some key scriptures of the promises of God.   First let me explain the difference between scriptural promises, and personal prophetic promises.

1. **Scripture promises:**

The Word of God is full of scriptures of promises to every believer but you have to activate the measure of faith God has given unto you in order to obtain that promise. (A promise can't do you any good if you never receive it). So let's receive all of God's promises. There are scripture promises of health in the Word of God. Isaiah 6:10

> *"Make the heart of this people fat, and make their eyes heavy, and shut their eyes; lest they see with their eyes, and hear with their ears, and understand with their heart, and convert, and be healed."*

Not only is this a promise, but a command to be healed.

2. Personal Prophetic Promises:

There have been many personal prophesies that have went forth. First, and foremost be sure it was from the Lord. Too many times the people of God think that they are hearing from God when actually they didn't. When it was spoken, did your spirit agree with what was said? Did it line up wit the Word of God?

Secondly, if God said it is definitely going to come to pass, whether it takes two weeks, two months or two years, you can expect to see God move. In most cases people don't have enough faith to believe God can bless them with things they never had before.

When doubt is present you won't receive anything from God.   Therefore satan snatches your blessing.   In order to receive the promise you have to believe God from the moment it's spoken until the very second you receive it no matter what the circumstances may look like.

People of God know that God is working in your behalf no matter what kind of a picture satan paints before your eyes.   Now then, people of God let me share this key scripture of promise:

> *"And I will give unto thee the KEYS of the King-*
> *dom of heaven: and whatsoever thou shalt bind*
> *on Earth shall be bound in heaven: and whatso-*
> *ever thou Shalt loose on earth shall be loosed in*
> *heaven."*

> —*Matt. 16:19*

Beloved ones so many times we acknowledge, oh yeah I know that scripture. Beloved get the scripture down in your spirit, because only then can the Word of God go out with power and accomplish what you speak it to go forth to do.   Nothing can be accomplished in your flesh.

The Word of God is powerful all by itself.   Therefore, if you get the Word in your spirit man there is no promise that satan can keep you from getting to. Many times we have the Word in our minds and not in our hearts, learn to receive the Word with your heart and spirit, and not just in your mind.   If you only receive it in your mind you can soon forget it before it gets planted deep within your spirit.

If you get it down in your spirit the Holy Ghost can always bring it back to your remembrance and use it at time of need.   If someone gives you a set of keys that means you have the right and author-ity to use them whenever you want, and as many times as you please.   So start using your keys to the Glory of God!

There are some key things God wants to share with his people.   In order for him to share these things he must use some willing and yielded vessels that are open to him.   God has formed some min-istries in this end-time that are especially anointed and equipped to share some unrevealed mysteries of the gospel with the Body of Christ.   They also are especially prepared to do battle in the realm of the spirit to war against satan.

There are unsearchable riches in him. Ephesians 3:8-10 says:

> *"Unto me, who less than the least of all saints, in this grace given, that I should preach among the Gentiles the unsearchable riches of Christ; And to make all men see what is the fellowship of the mystery, which from the beginning of the world hath been hid in God, who created all things by Jesus Christ: To the intent that now unto the principalites and powers in heavenly places might*

be known by the church the manifold wisdom of God,"

My friend by the great power of travail and intercession we will begin to see these things come to pass. We must begin to understand that God and only God has predestinated and ordained different ministries before the foundation of the world.

Jesus also promised that he is coming quickly *Revelations 22:7, "Behold, I come quickly: blessed is he that keepeth the sayings of the prophecy of this book."* This is another promise beloved ones Jesus is coming soon, he is coming quickly. *"Watch and pray: for ye know not when the time is." (Mark 13:33)* Jesus has commanded all that we are watchful and prayerful, if we don't do what has been commanded we are subject to miss Jesus.

Beloved, every written word was a warning that we all should watch for his coming.

"He which testifieth these things saith, surely I come quickly. Amen. Even so, come Lord Jesus."

—Revelation 22:20

Conclusion

The anointing of the Last Hour shall be greater and powerful in this hour than any has seen in the history of the church. The anointing of the Last Hour shall be as it were in the days of the Apostles. It will to a degree, measure far above that which is believable.

It will be unbelievable because in this day and time the people have not seen God move to that extreme. The anointing of the Last Hour shall rest upon the people of God like never before. Yokes and heavy bands shall be broken. People that have suffered from different bondages will be set free. Soul ties of all types will be broken. People that thought they would never be free will receive salvation and great deliverance. And the glory of

God shall rest upon the people of God in the last hour. The glory of the Lord shall appear over the glorious church in the last hour, because Jehovah God, the Messiah is coming back for the glorious church. The glory of the Lord shall hover over the nation as the people of God rejoice as they receive their King! Thus said The Lord.

A Prayer of Repentance for the Nation

Dear God, I pray for this land and country America, stand beside her and forgive her for all her sins. Forgive America for the many laws of iniquity that we have passed against you. Forgive America oh God for not allowing our precious children to pray freely in our schools. Forgive us oh God for destroying the trillions of unborn babies that we slaughter every year. Forgive us oh God for taking the ten commandments out of the court houses forgive America oh god for coming against righteous Holy leaders who take a stand in the name of God to stand against all those who are evil. And above all God forgive this land and country of American for its idols and idol worshippers. Forgive us for worshipping people and things above you. And Lord God help this land of ours, and help the many child abusers and sex offenders to come to repentance. Our God we pray as a nation right now that you would help America and guide her back to what is right and holy. Ooh Lord we ask that you would have mercy on this land that we call America and please oh God let your hand of judgement not come down on us. Oh God let it not be as those days when there was no king in Israel: and every man did that which was right in his own eyes. Forgive America we pray oh God for the many men who have left the natural use of a woman and burn in their own lust to lay with another man. Forgive us oh God for the many women who have left the natural use of a man and desire to lay with another woman. Oh take our hands now we pray thee and guide us back to you. That we may find grace and mercy in your sight oh God for it is only you who we now seek to please. We thank thee oh God for how you have suffered long with America. Forgive us oh God for the many lies we have told. And for taking things that did not belong to us, forgive us for being a thief on our jobs. Stealing time by never showing up on time, forgive us oh God for helping ourselves to the many office supplies we have put in our purses and walked away as if it belonged to us. Forgive all of us oh God who enjoys all the sins of the flesh, who enjoy drunkenness, and elicit drug use of every kind trying to forget our troubles. All we need to do as a nation is turn our face to you and you will forgive this land we can America and heal it from its disease. And for this oh great God Jehovah we thank thee for allowing us as a nation to pray this prayer of repentance in the name of Jesus thou great son of King David. Now Lord I ask that you will fill me with your sweet Holy Spirit fill me with Holy Ghost fire and never, ever, ever let me be the same again. Amen and Amen and Amen...

A Prayer of Repentance

"That if thou shall confess with thy mouth The Lord Jesus, and shall believe in thine heart that God Hath raised him from the dead, thou shall be saved."

—*Romans 10:9*

Lord Jesus come into my heart. Forgive me for all of my sins. Lord Jesus show me how to walk in the light of your Word. Lord Jesus I desire to walk in holiness and sanctification. I pray that you would create in me a clean heart. Lord Jesus I ask that you help me to put on the mind of Christ. Father God I pray that you would renew my mind daily with righteousness. Lord Jesus I thank you for saving me. Lord Jesus I thank you for my salvation.

A Prayer of Rededication

"With my whole heart have I sought thee: O let Me not wander from thy commandments."

—*Psalms 119:10*

Lord I pray that you would rededicate me. I ask forgiveness for not being totally dedicated to you. Lord Jesus I desire to seek you with my whole heart, so that I won't wonder from your commandments. Lord God I realize that carnality is not pleasing in your eyesight. Lord Jesus teach me the way of your statue, and show me how to truly walk in the spirit. Lord Jesus I now thank you and praise your holy name for my rededication.

A Pray of
Commitment

"To wit, that God was in Christ, reconciling The world unto himself, not imputing their trespasses unto them; And hath committed unto us the Word of reconciliation."

—*II Corinthians 5:19*

Lord Jesus I now ask forgiveness for not being committed to you, and not being committed to the Word.   Lord Jesus I desire to become totally committed to your Word.   Lord Jesus I pray that you would renew my fellowship and devotion to you.   I pray that you would help me to use my stumbling blocks as stepping-stones.   Lord Jesus I also pray that you would teach me how to glory in my tribulations, that I might learn that tribulations

can be used as a strengthening process in my commitment to you.   Lord Jesus I now thank you and
praise you for renewing my commitment to you.

About the book and author

The Return of Jesus Christ was written out of the inspiration of the Holy Spirit. It was written to inspire men and women everywhere to focus upon the return of Jesus Christ.

At the age of 18 Evangelist Adrienne Manson received her calling from the Lord. God has commissioned her as a ministry gift to operate as an Apostle to birth out other ministry gifts and to train them effectively and to stir up the gift which is within them. Evangelist Manson is founder of Zoë Ministries P.O. Box 24935, Chicago, IL 60624.

You may contact Evangelist Manson for speaking engagements, seminars, or training classes on intercessory prayer; classes are also offered for those who feel they have gifts within them and need to be birthed forth. The Lord has anointed Evangelist Manson to call those gifts forth and to activate them within your personal life. I feel there are far too many Christians who have gifts, but don't know what they are; or don't know how to use them. It is the place and job of the leaders to take their rightful position and guide the body into the right position so that we may form a mighty army and to go in and inherit the land, and live victorious lives.

There is a changing of the guards taking place the Moses of this generation have died, and now God is raising up the Joshua Leaders to help the Body of Christ cross over this Jordan and possess the promise land.

It is the vision of Zoë Ministries to equip, assist, train, and build up the believer to operate at a level of authority, and to take back what belongs to you. For more information you may write P.O. Box 24935, Chicago, IL 60624.

Printed in the United Kingdom
by Lightning Source UK Ltd.
121466UK00001BA/19/A